THIS BOOK BELONGS TO

START DATE

MONTH | DAY | YEAR

SHE READS TRUTH™

© 2017 She Reads Truth, LLC
All rights reserved.

ISBN 978-1-946282-10-1

No part of this publication may be reproduced, distributed, or transmitted in any form or by any means, including photocopying, recording, or other electronic or mechanical methods, without the prior written permission of She Reads Truth, LLC, except in the case of brief quotations embodied in critical reviews and certain other noncommercial uses permitted by copyright law.

Unless otherwise noted, all Scripture is taken from the Christian Standard Bible®, Copyright © 2017 by Holman Bible Publishers. Used by permission. Christian Standard Bible® and CSB® are federally registered trademarks of Holman Bible Publishers.

Photography © 2017 by Risha Chesterfield (40, 60) and Rachel Moore (cover, 12, 18, 22, 32, 46, 50, 56). Used by permission.

James

TRUE RELIGION

SHE READS TRUTH

Nashville, Tennessee

In a style that is as gracious as it is unflinching, as uplifting as it is unapologetic, James paints a picture of true religion—a faith not just of hearing but of doing.

EDITOR'S LETTER

G. K. Chesterton wrote, "It has often been said, very truly, that religion is the thing that makes the ordinary man feel extraordinary." From what I've observed, I agree.

It's hard to deny that we all long to connect with something greater, better, and beyond ourselves, and when we find that something, it is an extraordinary feeling—a good kind of different. But is this all religion is for?

Chesterton goes on to say: "it is an equally important truth that religion is the thing that makes the extraordinary man feel ordinary." Okay, now we're getting somewhere. True religion does not simply make me feel connected to something greater than myself; it actually changes me from the inside out.

This change requires humility, and it very often requires surrender. These feelings are not always pleasant, but they are necessary. And I wonder, can true religion—the religion God delights in—exist apart from them?

The priest in Jesus' parable of the Good Samaritan had religion, but when he saw an assaulted man lying injured in a ditch, he passed him by. Saul had religion before he became Paul, while he was persecuting Christ followers and standing by at their stoning. Today there are religious men and women populating pews around the world, and perhaps we sit among them. Perhaps we are them. How do we know if our own religion is true, pleasing to our Creator?

James's letter is packed full of practical, wisdom-filled instruction for the believer—deeply convicting details of how the Christ-follower is to live the redeemed life. He offers insight on how to pray, how to follow the Lord through seasons of trial, and how to speak in ways that honor others. In a style that is as gracious as it is unflinching, as uplifting as it is unapologetic, James paints a picture of true religion—a faith not just of hearing but of doing.

Our team has included some beautiful and helpful resources in this study book to help us sweep a magnifying glass across this text written by Jesus' own brother. The map shows the probable circulation of James's original letter among the Jewish and Gentile believers of his time. We've also created a chart to illustrate how Jesus' teaching echoes throughout the book of James, which is especially fascinating since we know from Scripture that James did not believe Jesus was the Messiah until after Jesus' earthly ministry (John 7:5). You'll find other interesting details listed on pages 16 and 17—bits of information about Jesus' immediate family that we can piece together from Scripture.

Before you begin your reading of James, ask the Holy Spirit to be your guide, illuminating the words He inspired long ago and actively works through today. Ask Him to guard you from the temptation to twist James's words into legalism or moralism, and to help you see Jesus more clearly as you read. I will do the same. May true religion make us feel both ordinary and extraordinary because of who Jesus is and what He has done.

Amanda

Amanda Bible Williams
EDITOR-IN-CHIEF

JAMES: TRUE RELIGION

The testing of your faith produces endurance

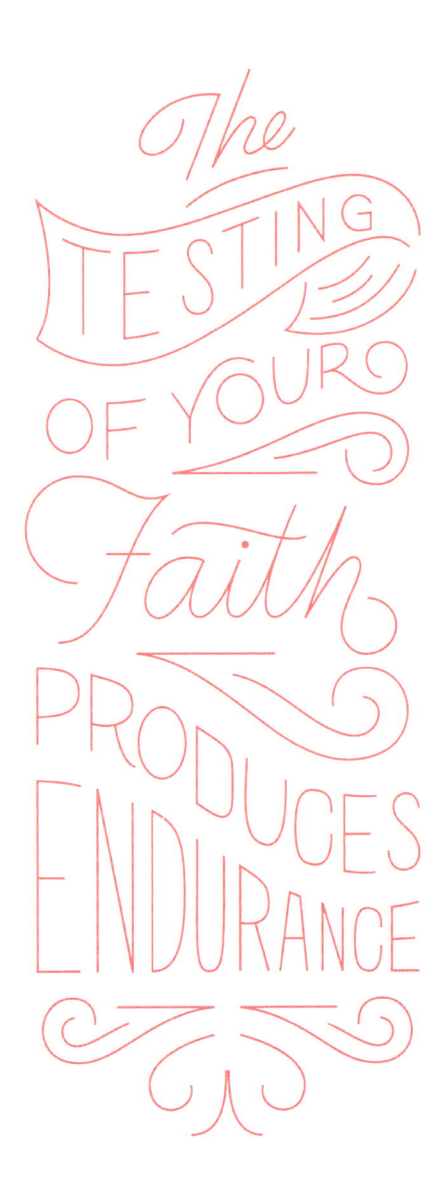

KEY VERSE

Consider it a great joy, my brothers and sisters, whenever you experience various trials, because you know that the testing of your faith produces endurance. And let endurance have its full effect, so that you may be mature and complete, lacking nothing. –JAMES 1:2-4

SHE READS JAMES

ON THE TIMELINE:

There is no information in James's letter to suggest a specific date, but scholars presume the writing took place between A.D. 48-52, ten or more years before James's death in A.D. 62 or 66.

A LITTLE BACKGROUND:

James, the brother of Jesus, is most likely the author of this epistle (Matthew 13:55; Mark 6:3; and Galatians 1:19). Though he was not a follower of Christ during Jesus' earthly ministry (John 7:3-5), a post-resurrection appearance convinced James that Jesus was indeed the Christ (Acts 1:14; 1 Corinthians 15:7). James later led the Jerusalem church (Galatians 2:9,12) and exercised great influence there (Acts 1:14; 21:18; 1 Corinthians 15:7; Galatians 2:9,12).

MESSAGE & PURPOSE:

As a general epistle, James was written to a broad audience rather than a specific group of people. James focuses on themes of wisdom, faith, and moral and ethical conduct. The author highlights wisdom as valuable for proper speech in worship (3:7-12), for determining who ought to teach (1:19-27; 3:1-8), and for avoiding internal conflicts within congregations (3:13-18; 4:1-12). He presents the importance of faith in action (1:19-27; 2:14-26), stating that faith which does not express itself in good works is useless (2:20). The epistle also deals with ethics and social justice (2:1-13; 4:1-12; 5:1-12).

Give Thanks for the Book of James:

James continually called for obedience to the law of God, showing believers that their obedience to God's moral standards was an indication of a living faith. Some choose to oversimplify the distinctions between the Old and New Testaments by saying that the Old Testament is grounded in works and the New Testament is grounded in faith. James brings both testaments together to show that faith and works are integrally related in both the old and new covenants.

HOW TO STUDY WITH THE ONLINE COMMUNITY

For added community, conversation, and devotionals, join us in the **James** reading plan on the She Reads Truth app or on SheReadsTruth.com— where women from Fresno to France will be reading along with you!

Have a "He" in your life—a brother, father, husband, friend? Invite him to join you by visiting HeReadsTruth.com or the He Reads Truth app, or by picking up the guy version of this book at ShopHeReadsTruth.com.

HOW TO USE THIS BOOK

She Reads Truth is a community of women dedicated to reading the Word of God every day. The Bible is living and active, breathed out by God, and we confidently hold it higher than anything we can do or say. This book focuses primarily on Scripture with helpful elements throughout.

SCRIPTURE READING

This study book includes the complete text of James, plus supplementary scriptures for fuller context.

HEAR & DO

Each day has writing prompts and journaling space to help you engage with the Truth you've read.

GRACE DAY

Use this day to catch up on your reading, pray, and rest in the presence of the Lord.

WEEKLY TRUTH

This day is set aside for weekly Scripture memorization.

DESIGN ON PURPOSE

The design of every She Reads Truth study book begins around a table. The SRT editorial team presents everything they've learned from studying a particular book of the Bible—James, in this case—while the creative team listens with eager ears. "Content drives creative" are the words we remember often, and as the creative department took the baton of *James: True Religion*, they did so with intention.

James's letter is alive with quick motion and concise truth. The photography in this book represents a woman who is actively "doing"—a nod to James's exhortation to be more than hearers of the Word, but to be doers also.

We used an invigorating orange throughout this book to underscore this idea of activity and alertness. We chose Frieght Display, a strong and grounded typeface, because in the midst of all this activity, the action comes from being grounded in the Word of God.

Designing this book together allowed our team to discuss real life applications of both hearing and doing. We gave you space for this as well—space to process and plan how you will be not just a hearer of the Word, but also a doer, to the glory of God.

16
JESUS' FAMILY

46
GRACE FOR THE HUMBLE

50
BOASTING ABOUT TOMORROW

table of contents

WEEK ONE

12	DAY 1 How Can We Rejoice in Suffering?
18	DAY 2 Both Hearing and Doing
22	DAY 3 Mercy Triumphs Over Judgment
26	DAY 4 Faith Made Complete
32	DAY 5 Controlling the Tongue
36	DAY 6 Grace Day
38	DAY 7 Weekly Truth

EXTRAS

16	INFOGRAPHIC Jesus' Family
30	CHART Echoes of Jesus in James
44	MAP Circulation of James's Original Letter
54	HYMN How Firm a Foundation
74	For the Record
80	Beauty, Goodness, and Truth

WEEK TWO

40	DAY 8 Wisdom from Above
46	DAY 9 Grace for the Humble
50	DAY 10 Boasting About Tomorrow
56	DAY 11 Warnings to the Rich
60	DAY 12 Patience for the Long Haul
64	DAY 13 Grace Day
66	DAY 14 Weekly Truth

11

WEEK ONE: DAY 1

How Can We Rejoice in Suffering?

James 1:1-18

GREETING

¹ James, a servant of God and of the Lord Jesus Christ:
To the twelve tribes dispersed abroad.

Greetings.

TRIALS AND MATURITY

² Consider it a great joy, my brothers and sisters, whenever you experience various trials, ³ because you know that the testing of your faith produces endurance. ⁴ And let endurance have its full effect, so that you may be mature and complete, lacking nothing.

⁵ Now if any of you lacks wisdom, he should ask God—who gives to all generously and ungrudgingly—and it will be given to him. ⁶ But let him ask in faith without doubting. For the doubter is like the surging sea, driven and tossed by the wind. ⁷ That person should not expect to receive anything from the Lord, ⁸ being double-minded and unstable in all his ways.

⁹ Let the brother of humble circumstances boast in his exaltation, ¹⁰ but let the rich boast in his humiliation because he will pass away like a flower of the field. ¹¹ For the sun rises and, together with the scorching wind, dries up the grass; its flower falls off, and its beautiful appearance perishes. In the same way, the rich person will wither away while pursuing his activities.

¹² Blessed is the one who endures trials, because when he has stood the test he will receive the crown of life that God has promised to those who love him.

¹³ No one undergoing a trial should say, "I am being tempted by God," since God is not tempted by evil, and he himself doesn't tempt anyone. ¹⁴ But each person is tempted when he is drawn away and enticed by his own evil desire. ¹⁵ Then after desire has conceived, it gives birth to sin, and when sin is fully grown, it gives birth to death.

¹⁶ Don't be deceived, my dear brothers and sisters. ¹⁷ Every good and perfect gift is from above, coming down from the Father of lights, who does not change like shifting shadows. ¹⁸ By his own choice, he gave us birth by the word of truth so that we would be a kind of firstfruits of his creatures.

Jeremiah 31:7-14

GOD'S PEOPLE BROUGHT HOME

⁷ For this is what the Lord says:

> Sing with joy for Jacob;
> shout for the foremost of the nations!
> Proclaim, praise, and say,
> "Lord, save your people,
> the remnant of Israel!"
> ⁸ Watch! I am going to bring them from the northern land.
> I will gather them from remote regions of the earth—
> the blind and the lame will be with them,
> along with those who are pregnant and those about to give birth.
> They will return here as a great assembly!
> ⁹ They will come weeping,
> but I will bring them back with consolation.
> I will lead them to wadis filled with water,
> by a smooth way where they will not stumble,
> for I am Israel's Father,
> and Ephraim is my firstborn.
> ¹⁰ Nations, hear the word of the Lord,
> and tell it among the far off coasts and islands!
> Say, "The one who scattered Israel will gather him.
> He will watch over him as a shepherd guards his flock,
> ¹¹ for the Lord has ransomed Jacob
> and redeemed him from the power of one stronger than he."
> ¹² They will come and shout for joy on the heights of Zion;
> they will be radiant with joy
> because of the Lord's goodness,
> because of the grain, the new wine, the fresh oil,
> and because of the young of the flocks and herds.
> Their life will be like an irrigated garden,
> and they will no longer grow weak from hunger.
> ¹³ Then the young women will rejoice with dancing,
> while young and old men rejoice together.
> I will turn their mourning into joy,
> give them consolation,
> and bring happiness out of grief.
> ¹⁴ I will refresh the priests with an abundance,
> and my people will be satisfied with my goodness.
>
> This is the Lord's declaration.

Matthew 4:1-11

THE TEMPTATION OF JESUS

¹ Then Jesus was led up by the Spirit into the wilderness to be tempted by the devil. ² After he had fasted forty days and forty nights, he was hungry. ³ Then the tempter approached him and said, "If you are the Son of God, tell these stones to become bread."

⁴ He answered, "It is written: Man must not live on bread alone but on every word that comes from the mouth of God."

⁵ Then the devil took him to the holy city, had him stand on the pinnacle of the temple, ⁶ and said to him, "If you are the Son of God, throw yourself down. For it is written:

> He will give his angels orders concerning you,
> and they will support you with their hands
> so that you will not strike
> your foot against a stone."

⁷ Jesus told him, "It is also written: Do not test the Lord your God."

⁸ Again, the devil took him to a very high mountain and showed him all the kingdoms of the world and their splendor. ⁹ And he said to him, "I will give you all these things if you will fall down and worship me."

¹⁰ Then Jesus told him, "Go away, Satan! For it is written: Worship the Lord your God, and serve only him."

¹¹ Then the devil left him, and angels came and began to serve him.

1 Peter 1:6-7

⁶ You rejoice in this, even though now for a short time, if necessary, you suffer grief in various trials ⁷ so that the proven character of your faith—more valuable than gold which, though perishable, is refined by fire—may result in praise, glory, and honor at the revelation of Jesus Christ.

Hear & Do

WHAT DOES THE PASSAGE SAY?

WHAT WILL I DO?

JAMES: TRUE RELIGION

Joseph, Mary's husband, seems to have died early. Most scholars assume this since he is never mentioned after the trip to Jerusalem Jesus took as a boy, described in Luke 2:41-51.

Jesus' Family

James was Jesus' half-brother, a natural born son of Mary and Joseph. The Bible is relatively silent about the first thirty years of Jesus' life, but when we piece together the details that are given, a fascinating picture of His immediate family begins to emerge. What else does the Bible tell us about Jesus' family?

James and Jesus' other brothers eventually believed. Paul tells us in 1 Corinthians 9:1-5 that not only did Jesus' brothers come to believe in Him, they became missionaries for the early Church.

SHE READS TRUTH

Jesus' disciples cared for Jesus' family after the resurrection. In John 19:27, Jesus calls on His disciple John to take over caring for Mary. Acts 1:13-14 describes the disciples coming alongside Jesus' mother and brothers after Jesus' crucifixion and resurrection.

Jesus came from a family of at least seven children. Matthew 13:55-56 says Jesus had four brothers whose names were James, Joseph, Simon, and Judas, and that He also had sisters (the plural indicates at least two).

Jesus was the oldest of His brothers and sisters. Matthew 1:25 and Luke 2:7 name Jesus as Mary's firstborn, and the entire nativity story emphasizes the virgin birth.

Jesus' own family thought He was out of His mind. Mark 3:21 says when Jesus' family saw the crowds that were gathering to see Him, they thought He was insane.

Before His resurrection, Jesus' brothers did not believe He was the Christ. John 7:5 makes this clear. This would have included James, the author of this epistle.

WEEK ONE: DAY 2

Both Hearing and Doing

James 1:19-27

HEARING AND DOING THE WORD

¹⁹ My dear brothers and sisters, understand this: Everyone should be quick to listen, slow to speak, and slow to anger,

²⁰ for human anger does not accomplish God's righteousness. ²¹ Therefore, ridding yourselves of all moral filth and the evil that is so prevalent, humbly receive the implanted word, which is able to save your souls.

²² But be doers of the word and not hearers only, deceiving yourselves. ²³ Because if anyone is a hearer of the word and not a doer, he is like someone looking at his own face in a mirror. ²⁴ For he looks at himself, goes away, and immediately forgets what kind of person he was. ²⁵ But the one who looks intently into the perfect law of freedom and perseveres in it, and is not a forgetful hearer but a doer who works—this person will be blessed in what he does.

²⁶ If anyone thinks he is religious without controlling his tongue, his religion is useless and he deceives himself. ²⁷ Pure and undefiled religion before God the Father is this: to look after orphans and widows in their distress and to keep oneself unstained from the world.

Proverbs 10:19

When there are many words, sin is unavoidable, but the one who controls his lips is prudent.

Ephesians 4:26-27

[26] Be angry and do not sin. Don't let the sun go down on your anger, [27] and don't give the devil an opportunity.

Romans 5:20

The law came along to multiply the trespass. But where sin multiplied, grace multiplied even more.

Hear & Do

WHAT DOES THE PASSAGE SAY?

WHAT WILL I DO?

WEEK ONE: DAY 3

Mercy Triumphs Over Judgment

James 2:1-13

THE SIN OF FAVORITISM

¹ My brothers and sisters, do not show favoritism as you hold on to the faith in our glorious Lord Jesus Christ. ² For if someone comes into your meeting wearing a gold ring and dressed in fine clothes, and a poor person dressed in filthy clothes also comes in, ³ if you look with favor on the one wearing the fine clothes and say, "Sit here in a good place," and yet you say to the poor person, "Stand over there," or "Sit here on the floor by my foot-stool," ⁴ haven't you made distinctions among yourselves and become judges with evil thoughts?

⁵ Listen, my dear brothers and sisters: Didn't God choose the poor in this world to be rich in faith and heirs of the kingdom that he has promised to those who love him? ⁶ Yet you have dishonored the poor. Don't the rich oppress you and drag you into court? ⁷ Don't they blaspheme the good name that was invoked over you?

⁸ Indeed, if you fulfill the royal law prescribed in the Scripture, Love your neighbor as yourself, you are doing well. ⁹ If, however, you show favoritism, you commit sin and are convicted by the law as transgressors. ¹⁰ For whoever keeps the entire law, and yet stumbles at one point, is guilty of breaking it all. ¹¹ For he who said, Do not commit adultery, also said, Do not murder. So if you do not commit adultery, but you murder, you are a lawbreaker.

¹² Speak and act as those who are to be judged by the law of freedom. ¹³ For judgment is without mercy to the one who has not shown mercy. Mercy triumphs over judgment.

Zechariah 7:9-10

⁹ "The Lord of Armies says this: 'Make fair decisions. Show faithful love and compassion to one another. ¹⁰ Do not oppress the widow or the fatherless, the resident alien or the poor, and do not plot evil in your hearts against one another.'"

Matthew 7:1-5

DO NOT JUDGE

¹ "Do not judge, so that you won't be judged. ² For you will be judged by the same standard with which you judge others, and you will be measured by the same measure you use. ³ Why do you look at the splinter in your brother's eye but don't notice the beam of wood in your own eye? ⁴ Or how can you say to your brother, 'Let me take the splinter out of your eye,' and look, there's a beam of wood in your own eye? ⁵ Hypocrite! First take the beam of wood out of your eye, and then you will see clearly to take the splinter out of your brother's eye."

Romans 13:8-10

LOVE, OUR PRIMARY DUTY

⁸ Do not owe anyone anything, except to love one another, for the one who loves another has fulfilled the law. ⁹ The commandments, Do not commit adultery; do not murder; do not steal; do not covet; and any other commandment, are summed up by this commandment: Love your neighbor as yourself.

¹⁰ Love does no wrong to a neighbor. Love, therefore, is the fulfillment of the law.

Hear & Do

WHAT DOES THE PASSAGE SAY?

WHAT WILL I DO?

WEEK ONE: DAY 4

Faith Made Complete

James 2:14-26

FAITH AND WORKS

[14] What good is it, my brothers and sisters, if someone claims to have faith but does not have works? Can such faith save him?

[15] If a brother or sister is without clothes and lacks daily food [16] and one of you says to them, "Go in peace, stay warm, and be well fed," but you don't give them what the body needs, what good is it?

[17] In the same way faith, if it doesn't have works, is dead by itself.

[18] But someone will say, "You have faith, and I have works." Show me your faith without works, and I will show you faith by my works. [19] You believe that God is one. Good! Even the demons believe—and they shudder.

[20] Senseless person! Are you willing to learn that faith without works is useless? [21] Wasn't Abraham our father justified by works in offering Isaac his son on the altar?

[22] You see that faith was active together with his works, and by works, faith was made complete,

[23] and the Scripture was fulfilled that says, Abraham believed God, and it was credited to him as righteousness, and he was called God's friend. [24] You see that a person is justified by works and not by faith alone. [25] In the same way, wasn't Rahab the prostitute also justified by works in receiving the messengers and sending them out by a different route?
[26] For just as the body without the spirit is dead, so also faith without works is dead.

Deuteronomy 6:4-5

⁴ Listen, Israel: The Lord our God, the Lord is one. ⁵ Love the Lord your God with all your heart, with all your soul, and with all your strength.

Romans 3:23-26

²³ For all have sinned and fall short of the glory of God. ²⁴ They are justified freely by his grace through the redemption that is in Christ Jesus. ²⁵ God presented him as an atoning sacrifice in his blood, received through faith, to demonstrate his righteousness, because in his restraint God passed over the sins previously committed. ²⁶ God presented him to demonstrate his righteousness at the present time, so that he would be righteous and declare righteous the one who has faith in Jesus.

Ephesians 2:8-10

⁸ For you are saved by grace through faith, and this is not from yourselves; it is God's gift — ⁹ not from works, so that no one can boast.

¹⁰ For we are his workmanship, created in Christ Jesus for good works, which God prepared ahead of time for us to do.

Hear & Do

WHAT DOES THE PASSAGE SAY?

WHAT WILL I DO?

Echoes of Jesus in James

The book of James is unlike any other book in the New Testament. While it reads like a letter, it often adopts the stark style of Proverbs, the rhetorical strength of an Old Testament prophet, and the structure of a sermon. Perhaps most notably is how the book of James mirrors Jesus' Sermon on the Mount, which would have been very familiar to James, the brother of Jesus.

SERMON ON THE MOUNT	JESUS' TEACHING	JAMES
MATTHEW 5:3	Those who don't amount to much by the world's standards should be glad, for God has honored them.	1:9
MATTHEW 5:3-4	When you humble yourself and realize your dependence on God, He will lift you up.	4:10
MATTHEW 5:7; 6:14	Be merciful to others, as God is merciful to you.	2:13
MATTHEW 5:9	Blessed are the peacemakers; they plant in peace and reap a harvest of goodness.	3:17-18
MATTHEW 5:11-12	Whenever trouble comes, be joyful.	1:2
MATTHEW 5:12	Be patient in suffering, as God's prophets were patient.	5:10
MATTHEW 5:22	Watch out for your anger; it can be dangerous.	1:20
MATTHEW 5:33-37	Be honest in your speech; just say a simple yes or no so that you will not sin.	5:12
MATTHEW 6:19	Treasures on earth will only rot away and be eaten by moths. Store up eternal treasures in heaven.	5:2-3
MATTHEW 6:24	Friendship with the world makes you an enemy of God.	4:4
MATTHEW 7:1-2	Don't speak evil against each other. If you do, you are criticizing God's law.	4:11
MATTHEW 7:7-12	Ask God and He will answer.	1:5; 5:15
MATTHEW 7:21-23	Your faith must express itself in your actions.	2:14-16

WEEK ONE: DAY 5

Controlling the Tongue

James 3:1-12

CONTROLLING THE TONGUE

¹ Not many should become teachers, my brothers, because you know that we will receive a stricter judgment. ² For we all stumble in many ways. If anyone does not stumble in what he says, he is mature, able also to control the whole body. ³ Now if we put bits into the mouths of horses so that they obey us, we direct their whole bodies. ⁴ And consider ships: Though very large and driven by fierce winds, they are guided by a very small rudder wherever the will of the pilot directs. ⁵ So too, though the tongue is a small part of the body, it boasts great things.

Consider how a small fire sets ablaze a large forest.

⁶ And the tongue is a fire. The tongue, a world of unrighteousness, is placed among our members. It stains the whole body, sets the course of life on fire, and is itself set on fire by hell. ⁷ Every kind of animal, bird, reptile, and fish is tamed and has been tamed by humankind, ⁸ but no one can tame the tongue. It is a restless evil, full of deadly poison. ⁹ With the tongue we bless our Lord and Father, and with it we curse people who are made in God's likeness. ¹⁰ Blessing and cursing come out of the same mouth. My brothers and sisters, these things should not be this way. ¹¹ Does a spring pour out sweet and bitter water from the same opening? ¹² Can a fig tree produce olives, my brothers and sisters, or a grapevine produce figs? Neither can a saltwater spring yield fresh water.

Genesis 1:26-27

²⁶ Then God said, "Let us make man in our image, according to our likeness. They will rule the fish of the sea, the birds of the sky, the livestock, the whole earth, and the creatures that crawl on the earth."

²⁷ So God created man in his own image;
he created him in the image of God;
he created them male and female.

Psalm 12

OPPRESSION BY THE WICKED

For the choir director: according to Sheminith.
A psalm of David.

¹ Help, LORD, for no faithful one remains;
the loyal have disappeared from the human race.
² They lie to one another;
they speak with flattering lips and deceptive hearts.
³ May the LORD cut off all flattering lips
and the tongue that speaks boastfully.
⁴ They say, "Through our tongues we have power;
our lips are our own—who can be our master?"

⁵ "Because of the devastation of the needy
and the groaning of the poor,
I will now rise up," says the LORD.
"I will provide safety for the one who longs for it."

⁶ The words of the LORD are pure words,
like silver refined in an earthen furnace,
purified seven times.

⁷ You, LORD, will guard us;
you will protect us from this generation forever.
⁸ The wicked prowl all around,
and what is worthless is exalted by the human race.

Matthew 12:36-37

³⁶ "I tell you that on the day of judgment people will have to account for every careless word they speak. ³⁷ For by your words you will be acquitted, and by your words you will be condemned."

Hear & Do

WHAT DOES THE PASSAGE SAY?

WHAT WILL I DO?

JAMES: TRUE RELIGION

GRACE DAY

WEEK ONE: DAY 6

Grace

SHE READS TRUTH

Take this day as an opportunity to catch up on your reading, pray, and rest in the presence of the Lord.

**I will turn their mourning into joy,
give them consolation,
and bring happiness out of grief.**

JEREMIAH 31:13

WEEKLY TRUTH

WEEK ONE: DAY 7

Memorizing Scripture is one of the best ways to carry God-breathed truth, instruction, and reproof wherever we go.

As we study James, we will memorize the book's key verses together, James 1:2-4. This week, we'll begin with the first part of the passage, which teaches us the paradoxical truth of rejoicing in suffering.

SHE READS TRUTH

Truth

Consider it a great joy, my brothers and sisters, whenever you experience various trials, because you know that the testing of your faith produces endurance.

JAMES 1:2-3

WEEK TWO: DAY 8

Wisdom from Above

James 3:13-18

THE WISDOM FROM ABOVE

¹³ Who among you is wise and understanding? By his good conduct he should show that his works are done in the gentleness that comes from wisdom. ¹⁴ But if you have bitter envy and selfish ambition in your heart, don't boast and deny the truth. ¹⁵ Such wisdom does not come down from above but is earthly, unspiritual, demonic.

¹⁶ For where there is envy and selfish ambition, there is disorder and every evil practice.

¹⁷ But the wisdom from above is first pure, then peace-loving, gentle, compliant, full of mercy and good fruits, unwavering, without pretense. ¹⁸ And the fruit of righteousness is sown in peace by those who cultivate peace.

GOING DEEPER

Proverbs 11:18

The wicked person earns an empty wage,
but the one who sows righteousness, a true reward.

Romans 12:9-21

CHRISTIAN ETHICS

⁹ Let love be without hypocrisy. Detest evil; cling to what is good. ¹⁰ Love one another deeply as brothers and sisters. Outdo one another in showing honor. ¹¹ Do not lack diligence in zeal; be fervent in the Spirit; serve the Lord. ¹² Rejoice in hope; be patient in affliction; be persistent in prayer. ¹³ Share with the saints in their needs; pursue hospitality. ¹⁴ Bless those who persecute you; bless and do not curse. ¹⁵ Rejoice with those who rejoice; weep with those who weep. ¹⁶ Live in harmony with one another. Do not be proud; instead, associate with the humble. Do not be wise in your own estimation. ¹⁷ Do not repay anyone evil for evil. Give careful thought to do what is honorable in everyone's eyes. ¹⁸ If possible, as far as it depends on you, live at peace with everyone. ¹⁹ Friends, do not avenge yourselves; instead, leave room for God's wrath, because it is written, Vengeance belongs to me; I will repay, says the Lord. ²⁰ But

> If your enemy is hungry, feed him.
> If he is thirsty, give him something to drink.
> For in so doing
> you will be heaping fiery coals on his head.

²¹ Do not be conquered by evil, but conquer evil with good.

Galatians 5:22-23

²² But the fruit of the Spirit is love, joy, peace, patience, kindness, goodness, faithfulness, ²³ gentleness, and self-control. The law is not against such things.

Hebrews 12:11

No discipline seems enjoyable at the time, but painful. Later on, however, it yields the peaceful fruit of righteousness to those who have been trained by it.

Hear & Do

WHAT DOES THE PASSAGE SAY?

WHAT WILL I DO?

Circulation of James's original letter

James's letter was likely written to Jewish Christian readers (James 1:1) and was read in the area of Judea first. It was eventually distributed throughout the ancient Mediterranean world. This map shows the letter's first recipients in A.D. 48-52 and how, as time passed, it eventually reached Christians all around the Mediterranean.

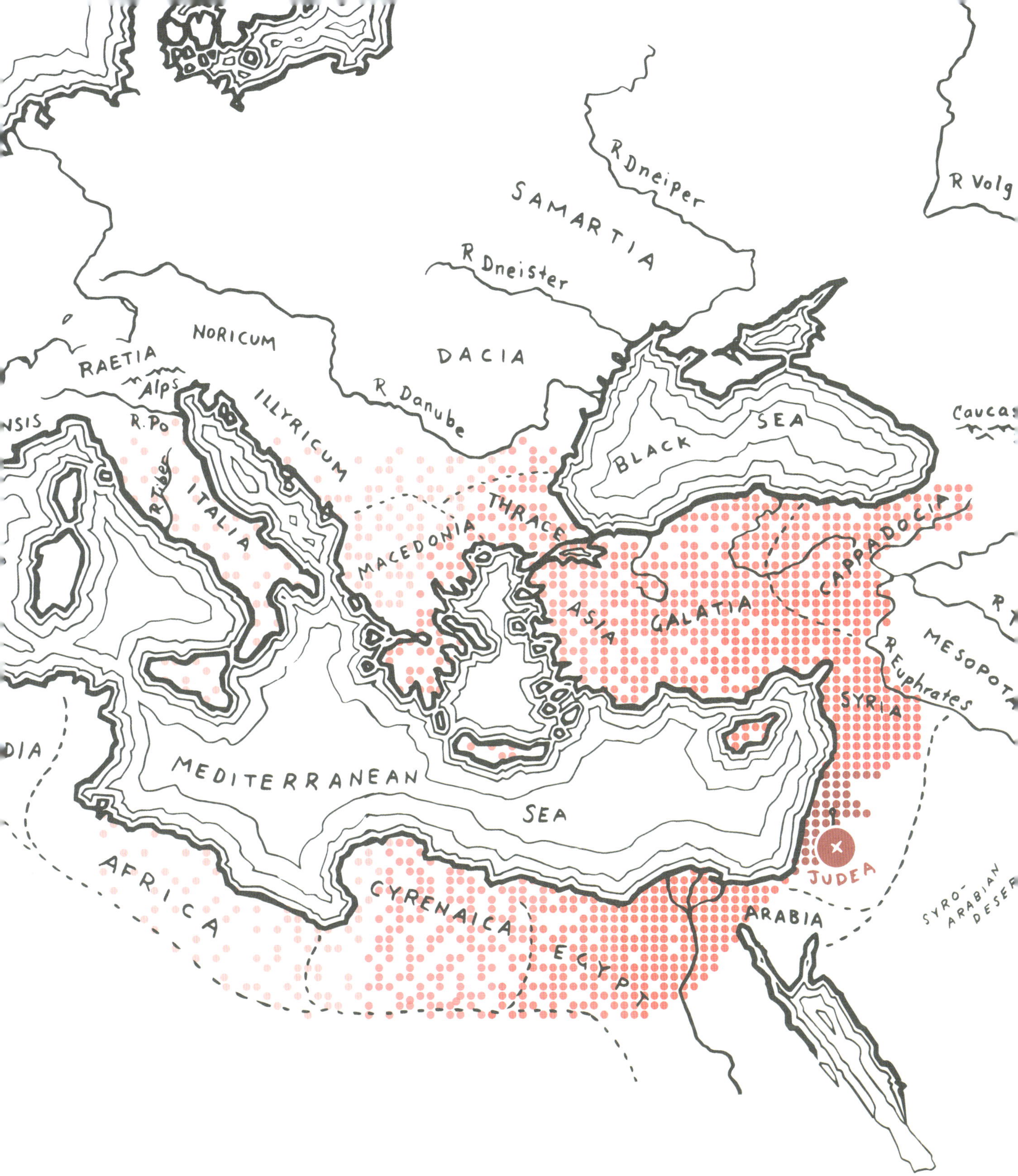
R Dneiper
SAMARTIA
R Volg
R Dneister
NORICUM
DACIA
RAETIA
Alps
R Danube
ILLYRICUM
NSIS
R.Po
R Tiber
ITALIA
BLACK SEA
Caucas
THRACE
MACEDONIA
CAPPADOCIA
ASIA
GALATIA
MESOPOTA
R Euphrates
SYRIA
DIA
MEDITERRANEAN SEA
JUDEA
AFRICA
CYRENAICA
ARABIA
SYRO-ARABIAN DESER
EGYPT

WEEK TWO: DAY 9

Grace for the Humble

James 4:1-12

PROUD OR HUMBLE

¹ What is the source of wars and fights among you? Don't they come from your passions that wage war within you? ² You desire and do not have. You murder and covet and cannot obtain. You fight and wage war. You do not have because you do not ask. ³ You ask and don't receive because you ask with wrong motives, so that you may spend it on your pleasures.

⁴ You adulterous people! Don't you know that friendship with the world is hostility toward God? So whoever wants to be the friend of the world becomes the enemy of God. ⁵ Or do you think it's without reason that the Scripture says: The spirit he made to dwell in us envies intensely?

⁶ But he gives greater grace. Therefore he says:

God resists the proud,
but gives grace to the humble.

⁷ Therefore, submit to God. Resist the devil, and he will flee from you. ⁸ Draw near to God, and he will draw near to you. Cleanse your hands, sinners, and purify your hearts, you double-minded. ⁹ Be miserable and mourn and weep. Let your laughter be turned to mourning and your joy to gloom. ¹⁰ Humble yourselves before the Lord, and he will exalt you.

¹¹ Don't criticize one another, brothers and sisters. Anyone who defames or judges a fellow believer defames and judges the law. If you judge the law, you are not a doer of the law but a judge. ¹² There is one lawgiver and judge who is able to save and to destroy. But who are you to judge your neighbor?

Psalm 9:19

Rise up, Lord! Do not let mere humans prevail;
let the nations be judged in your presence.

John 4:23-24

[23] "But an hour is coming, and is now here, when the true worshipers will worship the Father in Spirit and in truth. Yes, the Father wants such people to worship him. [24] God is spirit, and those who worship him must worship in Spirit and in truth."

Galatians 1:10

For am I now trying to persuade people, or God? Or am I striving to please people? If I were still trying to please people, I would not be a servant of Christ.

1 John 5:13-15

[13] I have written these things to you who believe in the name of the Son of God so that you may know that you have eternal life.

[14] This is the confidence we have before him:

If we ask anything according to his will, he hears us.

[15] And if we know that he hears whatever we ask, we know that we have what we have asked of him.

Hear & Do

WHAT DOES THE PASSAGE SAY?

WHAT WILL I DO?

WEEK TWO: DAY 10

Boasting About Tomorrow

James 4:13-17

OUR WILL AND GOD'S WILL

¹³ Come now, you who say, "Today or tomorrow we will travel to such and such a city and spend a year there and do business and make a profit." ¹⁴ Yet you do not know what tomorrow will bring— what your life will be!

> For you are like vapor that appears for a little while, then vanishes.

¹⁵ Instead, you should say, "If the Lord wills, we will live and do this or that." ¹⁶ But as it is, you boast in your arrogance. All such boasting is evil. ¹⁷ So it is sin to know the good and yet not do it.

Proverbs 27:1

Don't boast about tomorrow,
for you don't know what a day might bring.

Acts 18:19-21

[19] When they reached Ephesus he left them there, but he himself entered the synagogue and debated with the Jews. [20] When they asked him to stay for a longer time, he declined, [21] but he said farewell and added, "I'll come back to you again, if God wills." Then he set sail from Ephesus.

1 Corinthians 5:6-8

[6] Your boasting is not good. Don't you know that a little leaven leavens the whole batch of dough? [7] Clean out the old leaven so that you may be a new unleavened batch, as indeed you are. For Christ our Passover lamb has been sacrificed. [8] Therefore, let us observe the feast, not with old leaven or with the leaven of malice and evil, but with the unleavened bread of sincerity and truth.

Hear & Do

WHAT DOES THE PASSAGE SAY?

WHAT WILL I DO?

How Firm a Foundation

TEXT: RIPPON'S SELECTION OF HYMNS, 1787
TUNE: FUNK'S GENUINE CHURCH MUSIC, 1832

1 How___ firm a foun - da - tion, you saints of the Lord,
2 "Fear___ not, I am with you, O be not dis - mayed,
3 "When___ through the deep wa - ters I call you to go,
4 "When___ through fie - ry tri - als your path - way shall lie,
5 "The___ soul that on Je - sus still leans for re - pose,
is___ laid for your faith in His ex - cel - lent Word!
for___ I am your God and will still give you aid;
the___ ri - vers of sor - row shall not o - ver - flow;
my___ grace, all suf - fi - cient, shall be your sup - ply;
I___ will not, I will not de - sert to its foes;
What more can He say than to you He has said,
I'll streng - then you, help you, and cause you to stand,
for I will be with you, your trou - bles to bless,
the flame shall not hurt you, I on - ly de - sign
that soul, though all hell should en - dea - vor to shake,
to___ you who for re - fuge to Je - sus have fled?
u - pheld by my right - eous, o - mni - po - tent hand.
and___ sanc - ti - fy to you your deep - est dis - tress.
your___ dross to con - sume, and your gold to re - fine.
I'll___ ne - ver, no ne - ver, no ne - ver for - sake!"

WEEK TWO: DAY 11

Warnings to the Rich

James 5:1-6

WARNING TO THE RICH

¹ Come now, you rich people, weep and wail over the miseries that are coming on you. ² Your wealth has rotted and your clothes are moth-eaten. ³ Your gold and silver are corroded, and their corrosion will be a witness against you and will eat your flesh like fire. You have stored up treasure in the last days.

⁴ Look! The pay that you withheld from the workers who mowed your fields cries out, and the outcry of the harvesters has reached the ears of the Lord of Hosts.

⁵ You have lived luxuriously on the earth and have indulged yourselves. You have fattened your hearts in a day of slaughter. ⁶ You have condemned, you have murdered the righteous, who does not resist you.

Matthew 5:38-42

GO THE SECOND MILE

[38] "You have heard that it was said, An eye for an eye and a tooth for a tooth. [39] But I tell you, don't resist an evildoer. On the contrary, if anyone slaps you on your right cheek, turn the other to him also. [40] As for the one who wants to sue you and take away your shirt, let him have your coat as well. [41] And if anyone forces you to go one mile, go with him two. [42] Give to the one who asks you, and don't turn away from the one who wants to borrow from you."

Hebrews 10:35-39

[35] So don't throw away your confidence, which has a great reward. [36] For you need endurance, so that after you have done God's will, you may receive what was promised.

> [37] For yet in a very little while,
> the Coming One will come and not delay.
> [38] But my righteous one will live by faith;
> and if he draws back,
> I have no pleasure in him.

[39] But we are not those who draw back and are destroyed, but those who have faith and are saved.

Revelation 20:11-15

THE GREAT WHITE THRONE JUDGMENT

[11] Then I saw a great white throne and one seated on it. Earth and heaven fled from his presence, and no place was found for them. [12] I also saw the dead, the great and the small, standing before the throne, and books were opened. Another book was opened, which is the book of life, and the dead were judged according to their works by what was written in the books. [13] Then the sea gave up the dead that were in it, and death and Hades gave up the dead that were in them; each one was judged according to their works. [14] Death and Hades were thrown into the lake of fire. This is the second death, the lake of fire. [15] And anyone whose name was not found written in the book of life was thrown into the lake of fire.

Hear & Do

WHAT DOES THE PASSAGE SAY?

WHAT WILL I DO?

WEEK TWO: DAY 12

Patience for the Long Haul

James 5:7-20

WAITING FOR THE LORD

⁷ Therefore, brothers and sisters, be patient until the Lord's coming. See how the farmer waits for the precious fruit of the earth and is patient with it until it receives the early and the late rains.

⁸ You also must be patient. Strengthen your hearts, because the Lord's coming is near.

⁹ Brothers and sisters, do not complain about one another, so that you will not be judged. Look, the judge stands at the door!

¹⁰ Brothers and sisters, take the prophets who spoke in the Lord's name as an example of suffering and patience. ¹¹ See, we count as blessed those who have endured. You have heard of Job's endurance and have seen the outcome that the Lord brought about—the Lord is compassionate and merciful.

TRUTHFUL SPEECH

¹² Above all, my brothers and sisters, do not swear, either by heaven or by earth or with any other oath. But let your "yes" mean "yes," and your "no" mean "no," so that you won't fall under judgment.

EFFECTIVE PRAYER

¹³ Is anyone among you suffering? He should pray. Is anyone cheerful? He should sing praises. ¹⁴ Is anyone among you sick? He should call for the elders of the church, and they are to pray over him, anointing him with oil in the name of the Lord. ¹⁵ The prayer of faith will save the sick person, and the Lord will raise him up; if he has committed sins, he will be forgiven. ¹⁶ Therefore, confess your sins to one another and pray for one another, so that you may be healed. The prayer of a righteous person is very powerful in its effect. ¹⁷ Elijah was a human being as we are, and he prayed earnestly that it would not rain, and for three years and six months it did not rain on the land. ¹⁸ Then he prayed again, and the sky gave rain and the land produced its fruit.

¹⁹ My brothers and sisters, if any among you strays from the truth, and someone turns him back, ²⁰ let that person know that whoever turns a sinner from the error of his way will save his soul from death and cover a multitude of sins.

Joel 2:23

Children of Zion, rejoice and be glad
in the Lord your God,
because he gives you the autumn rain
for your vindication.
He sends showers for you,
both autumn and spring rain as before.

Matthew 5:33-37

TELL THE TRUTH

33 "Again, you have heard that it was said to our ancestors, You must not break your oath, but you must keep your oaths to the Lord. 34 But I tell you, don't take an oath at all: either by heaven, because it is God's throne; 35 or by the earth, because it is his footstool; or by Jerusalem, because it is the city of the great King. 36 Do not swear by your head, because you cannot make a single hair white or black. 37 But let your 'yes' mean 'yes,' and your 'no' mean 'no.' Anything more than this is from the evil one."

Hebrews 11:32-40

32 And what more can I say? Time is too short for me to tell about Gideon, Barak, Samson, Jephthah, David, Samuel, and the prophets, 33 who by faith conquered kingdoms, administered justice, obtained promises, shut the mouths of lions, 34 quenched the raging of fire, escaped the edge of the sword, gained strength in weakness, became mighty in battle, and put foreign armies to flight. 35 Women received their dead, raised to life again. Other people were tortured, not accepting release, so that they might gain a better resurrection. 36 Others experienced mockings and scourgings, as well as bonds and imprisonment. 37 They were stoned, they were sawed in two, they died by the sword, they wandered about in sheepskins, in goatskins, destitute, afflicted, and mistreated. 38 The world was not worthy of them. They wandered in deserts and on mountains, hiding in caves and holes in the ground.

39 All these were approved through their faith, but they did not receive what was promised, 40 since God had provided something better for us, so that they would not be made perfect without us.

1 Peter 4:7-11

END-TIME ETHICS

7 The end of all things is near; therefore, be alert and sober-minded for prayer. 8 Above all, maintain constant love for one another, since love covers a multitude of sins. 9 Be hospitable to one another without complaining. 10 Just as each one has received a gift, use it to serve others, as good stewards of the varied grace of God. 11 If anyone speaks, let it be as one who speaks God's words;

if anyone serves, let it be from the strength God provides, so that God may be glorified through Jesus Christ in everything.

To him be the glory and the power forever and ever. Amen.

Hear & Do

WHAT DOES THE PASSAGE SAY?

WHAT WILL I DO?

JAMES: TRUE RELIGION

GRACE DAY

WEEK TWO: DAY 13

Grace

SHE READS TRUTH

Take this day as an opportunity to catch up on your reading, pray, and rest in the presence of the Lord.

But the fruit of the Spirit is love, joy, peace, patience, kindness, goodness, faithfulness, gentleness, and self-control. The law is not against such things.

GALATIANS 5:22-23

WEEKLY TRUTH

WEEK TWO: DAY 14

Memorizing Scripture is one of the best ways to carry God-breathed truth, instruction, and reproof wherever we go.

As we study James, we are memorizing the book's key verses together, James 1:2-4. This week, we'll memorize verse 4, which focuses on the effect of enduring in Christ.

SHE READS TRUTH

Truth

And let endurance have its full effect, so that you may be mature and complete, lacking nothing.

JAMES 1:4

JAMES: TRUE RELIGION

It has often been said, very truly, that religion is the thing that makes the ordinary man feel extraordinary; it is an equally important truth that religion is the thing that makes the extraordinary man feel ordinary.

G. K. CHESTERTON

Notes

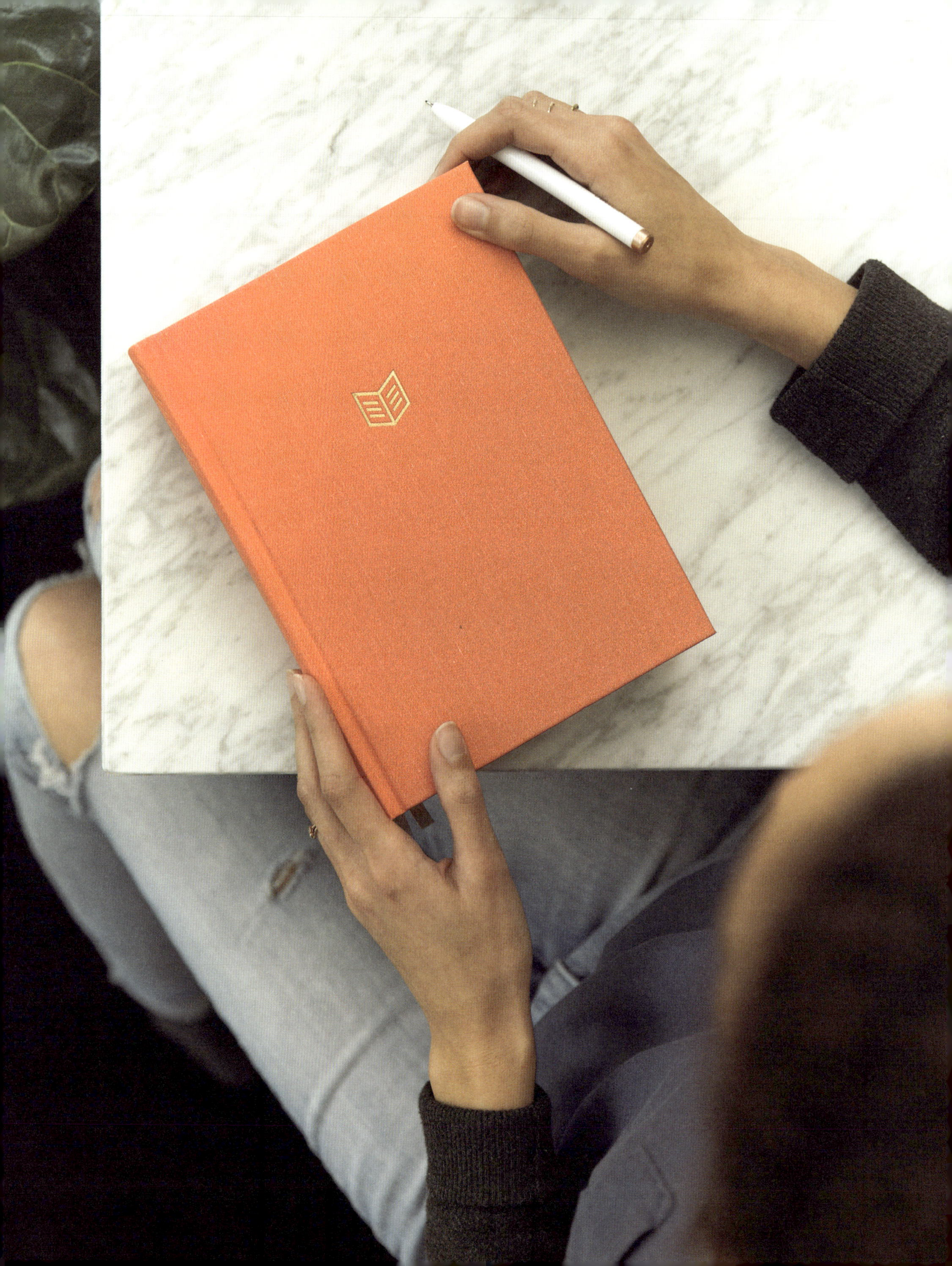

INHERENTLY BEAUTIFUL.
INTENTIONALLY DESIGNED.

Over two years ago, the She Reads Truth team set out to design a Bible that lends the inherently beautiful gospel the aesthetic beauty it deserves, while also offering in one place all the study tools the She Reads Truth community has grown to love.

INTRODUCING THE

SHE READS TRUTH BIBLE

featuring the Christian Standard Bible® (CSB) translation.

The *She Reads Truth Bible* features introductions and Scripture reading plans for each book of the Bible, with supplemental passages for deeper understanding; 66 artfully designed key verses; full-color maps, charts, and timelines; 189 devotionals by the She Reads Truth writing team; wide margins for journaling and note-taking, and more. It is a Bible designed with you in mind—to invite you to count yourself among the She Reads Truth community of "Women in the Word of God every day."

This is not a Bible for your shelf.
It is a Bible for your life.

———

SHEREADSTRUTHBIBLE.COM

SHE READS TRUTH | BIBLE

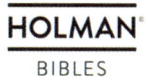

HOLMAN
BIBLES

FOR THE RECORD

Where did I study?

- ○ HOME
- ○ CHURCH
- ○ OFFICE
- ○ A FRIEND'S HOUSE
- ○ COFFEE SHOP
- ○ OTHER

DID I LISTEN TO MUSIC?

ARTIST:

SONG:

SCRIPTURE I WILL SHARE WITH A FRIEND:

WHEN DID I HAVE MY BEST STUDYING SUCCESS?

WHAT WAS HAPPENING IN THE WORLD?

What was my best takeaway?

WHAT WAS MY BIGGEST FEAR?

What was my greatest comfort?

I LEARNED THESE UNEXPECTED NEW THINGS:

1

2

3

END DATE

| MONTH | DAY | YEAR |

COLOPHON

This book was printed offset in Nashville, Tennessee, on 80# Lynx Opaque. Typefaces used include Freight Display, Garamond, and Euclid. Cover is printed offset on Tango 15 pt C1S with a soft-touch matte laminate. Finished size is 8"x10".

EDITORS-IN-CHIEF: Raechel Myers and Amanda Bible Williams

MANAGING EDITOR: Rebecca Faires

EDITORS: Russ Ramsey and Kara Gause

CREATIVE DIRECTOR: Ryan Myers

ART DIRECTOR: Amanda Barnhart

PRODUCTION DESIGN: Kelsea Allen

THEOLOGICAL OVERSIGHT:
Russ Ramsey, MDiv., ThM.
and Nate Shurden, MDiv.

COVER PHOTOGRAPHER: Rachel Moore

PHOTOGRAPHY: Risha Chesterfield and Rachel Moore

MAP: Caleb Faires

EDITORIAL INTERN: Ellen Taylor

SUBSCRIPTION INQUIRIES:
orders@shereadstruth.com

She Reads Truth is a worldwide community of women who
read God's Word together every day.

Founded in 2012, She Reads Truth invites women of all ages
to engage with Scripture through daily reading plans, online
conversation led by a vibrant community of contributors,
and offline resources created at the intersection of beauty,
goodness, and Truth.

STOP BY
shereadstruth.com

SHOP
shopshereadstruth.com

KEEP IN TOUCH
@shereadstruth

DOWNLOAD THE APP

SEND A NOTE
hello@shereadstruth.com

CONNECT
#SheReadsTruth

INTERSECTION OF **BEAUTY, GOODNESS, AND TRUTH**

Beauty

The She Reads Truth creative team is fueled by a singular objective: to lend the inherently beautiful gospel the aesthetic beauty it deserves. The studio photos of the newly released **She Reads Truth Bible** do exactly that. Freshly cut ranunculus, thistle, lamb's ear, and poppies made the perfect, naturally stunning backdrop to these special Bibles. You can see more photos from this series—and learn more about these brand new Bibles that are as beautiful inside as they are out—at SheReadsTruthBible.com.

Goodness

The phrase "**simple joy**" has been floating around #SRThq lately as we talk about the little things that make us happy. For some, it's a brand new set of pencils. For others, a coffee run at 2pm. And for almost all of us, it's a phone call from someone we love or a handwritten card from a faraway friend. Ask the people closest to you about their simple joys. Maybe you can bring them a little extra happiness in the coming weeks.

SEND A NOTE   hello@shereadstruth.com

IJM

Speaking of faith in action, our friends at **International Justice Mission** are responding in a very tangible way to God's call to love and seek justice for all people. IJM is an organization that protects the poor from violence in developing parts of the world. Their team includes more than 750 lawyers, investigators, social workers, and other professionals at work through seventeen field offices around the globe. To date, IJM has rescued more than 32,000 people from slavery… and counting. Consider becoming a Freedom Partner at IJM.org.

& Truth